MOM CAN

"A DEVOTIONAL AND JOURNAL FOR MOMS"

written by
Emmie R Werner

art by
Jack Foster

Halo
PUBLISHING
INTERNATIONAL

Halo
PUBLISHING
INTERNATIONAL

Halo Publishing International
8000 W Interstate 10, #600
San Antonio, Texas 78230

First Edition, April 2023
ISBN: 978-1-63765-374-6
Library of Congress Control Number: 2023902147

Halo Publishing International is a self-publishing company that publishes adult fiction and non-fiction, children's literature, self-help, spiritual, and faith-based books. We continually strive to help authors reach their publishing goals and provide many different services that help them do so. We do not publish books that are deemed to be politically, religiously, or socially disrespectful, or books that are sexually provocative, including erotica. Halo reserves the right to refuse publication of any manuscript if it is deemed not to be in line with our principles. Do you have a book idea you would like us to consider publishing? Please visit www.halopublishing.com for more information.

MOM CAN is dedicated to two of the best moms I know—Rita Willhelm, my mom, and Marie Werner, my husband's mom. An entire book could be written about them. Between them, they had one hundred years of marriage and fifty-five grandchildren! Their love for God and family was lived out each and every day of their lives.

They were wonderful examples to me...and to my children...and now to their children. They lived selfless lives of giving, either of their time or of something delicious from their kitchens. Family, friends, neighbors, or even strangers were blessed by them. What a lasting legacy! I am sure they didn't think of themselves as important or special, but to me they were.

My prayer is that at the end of MOM CAN, you CAN see yourself as special to your family and how special you are to God.

DAY 1

I can do all things [which He has called me to do] through Him who strengthens and empowers me [to fulfill His purpose—I am self-sufficient in Christ's sufficiency; I am ready for anything and equal to anything through Him who infuses me with strength and confident peace.]
(Philippians 4:13, Amplified Bible)

"Mom, can I have a cookie?"

"Mom, can I go play with Sam?"

"Mom, can I have five dollars?"

"Mom, can I have the car?"

"Mom, can I...?"

Well, you get the point. From the time they are little, a mom takes care of her children as their little needs grow to be big needs. When I read this scripture, I think, WOW, *He is everything I need. I can be the mom He has called me to be because He is in me and fills me with His strength and peace.*

Journal

Make a list of all the times you have seen Christ's sufficiency in your life and in your family.

Remember:

"I can do all things through Him who makes me strong."

Day 2

And this same God who takes care of me will supply all your needs from His glorious riches, which have been given to us in Christ Jesus. (Philippians 4:19, New Living Translation)

As Moms, we know how to care. When put to the test, we step up to care for family, parents, friends, neighbors, and even stray cats and dogs! When faced with a decision to care, even though we run the risk of a broken heart, we still say yes. Philippians tells us God takes care of us. What a comfort!

As we care for those we love, even a lost or stray cat or dog, God is caring for us. We care for His people, He cares for us. And so it goes...on and on.

Journal

Can you think of a time He asked you to care for someone or something and you were hesitant?

Remember:

"The same God who takes care of me will supply all my needs."

Day 3

> Because of the grace that God gave me, I can say to each one of you: don't think of yourself more highly than you ought to think. Instead, be reasonable since God has measured out a portion of faith to each one of you. (Romans 12:3, Common English Bible)

When I see Moms with little ones, I always smile and think, *ah, how sweet, so cute, and adorable.* Then I think back, *oh, I do remember the reality of being a brand-new mom, or the mom of toddlers and preschoolers.*

As children grow, they believe Moms can do everything–*Mom can play with me; Mom can help me; Mom can do it; Mom can take me.* And a million other *"Mom cans"* a mom fits into her day...only to do it all again the next day.

I think God was thinking of Moms when He said, "Because of the grace God gave me." A double portion to Moms, please.

Journal

Thank Him for His grace. Where do you see grace in your life?

Remember:

"God has measured out a portion of faith to each one of you."

Day 4

> Be strong like that, because God has given us His Spirit. And His Spirit does not cause us to be afraid. Instead, He causes us to be strong to serve God. He helps us to love God and other people. And He helps us to rule ourselves properly. (2 Timothy 1:7, Easy English Bible, 2018)

I was going to talk about how we as Moms have to watch and not be afraid. How many times in a day do we say to our kids, even our big kids, "Be careful, so you don't get hurt"? But the last sentence of this Bible passage stopped me in my tracks–"He helps us to rule ourselves properly."

That made me stop and think. If we allow Him to guide our entire life, our world, that means our choices will be made according to His word. We won't fear for our children because we are being ruled according to His word.

A novel thought? No, a GODLY thought.

Journal

In what areas do you need His help to rule yourself properly?

Remember:

"He helps us to rule ourselves properly."

Day 5

But those who know God and obey Him will be strong. They will fight back. (Daniel 11:32, Easy-to-Read Version)

Lunches packed, laundry finished and put away, forms filled out, and everyone tucked into bed. God is saying to you, "Yes, I see you are strong; you are obedient. I love you. Be still. Sit awhile with me."

Journal

Sit still with Him for five minutes...ten minutes. Tell Him how it makes you feel to stop and be with Him.

Remember:

"Those who obey God will be strong."

Day 6

But you belong to God, my dear children. You have already won a victory over those people, because the Spirit who lives in you is greater than the spirit who lives in the world. (I John, 4:4, New Living Translation)

You have already won the victory! You might say, "You have no idea what I am facing." Preschoolers who want your attention 24/7. Teens who don't want your attention, but in reality they do, an older family member, husband, or just life in general. All of them want your attention. When it's all piled together, it seems overwhelming.

Stop. Speak the Word of God into your life. Say, "I have victory over _____ (you fill in the blank) because greater is the Spirit in me than the spirit of the world." YES!

Journal

Write down your victories.

Remember:

"Greater is He that is in you. You have the victory."

Day 7

Now, thanks be to God who always causes us to triumph in Christ and through us reveals the fragrance of His knowledge in every place. (2 Corinthians 2:14, Modern English Version)

How many moms at the end of the day do a triumph dance? Or even have the energy to dance? Or, beat themselves up over what-ifs?

But that's not what God's word says. Let me paraphrase: "God always causes Moms to triumph!" So at the end of the day, do a triumph dance. You deserve it. You earned it!

Journal

What causes you to dance at the end of the day?

Day 8

For I was hungry and you fed me. I was thirsty and you gave me a drink. (Matthew 25:35, New Living Translation)

In God's eyes, there are no ordinary people. Each of us is His unique creation, made by Him for His purpose.

Maybe right now you are in the midst of changing diapers, doing laundry, feeding the hungry... and it will start all over again tomorrow. You are not an ordinary mom. You are a beautiful woman created by Him for such a time as this.

Journal

Make a list of the ways God made you unique.

Remember:

"I was hungry and you fed me. I was thirsty and you gave me a drink."

Day 9

Here's another way to put it: You're here to be light, bringing out the God-colors in the world. God is not a secret to be kept. (Matthew 5:14-15, The Message)

What are your gifts? Do you feel as if they are not being used in this season of your life? God did not give you talents just so they can be hidden under a basket.

Take a serious look at your talents and passions. How can you use them for His kingdom? Remember, your mission field is right there in your home, around your table. Oh, the joy you find in using your God-given talents! Oh, the joy your family reaps!

Journal

List His gifts and talents in your life.

Remember:

"You're here to be a light, bringing out the God-colors in the world."

Day 10

If you don't know what you're doing, pray to the Father. He loves to help. You'll get His help, and won't be condescended to when you ask for it. Ask boldly, believingly, without second thought. (James 1:5-6, The Message)

I used to say, when our girls were little, that I wished they had come with an instruction manual. I can't tell you how many times I said that over the years...until I had a revelation. They did come with instructions–His Holy Bible.

His word tells us how to raise our kids, how to be good parents, and how to discipline. Imagine that! God thought of everything when He created the universe...and me...and YOU!

Journal

List some of your concerns as a parent, and then search His word for His answers.

Remember:

"If you don't know what you are doing, pray to the Father."

Day 11

It is because of God's work that you now belong to Christ Jesus. As a result of Christ's death on the cross, we share in God's wise plan. (I Corinthians 1:30, Easy English Bible, 2018)

How many times did you ask for wisdom today? Wisdom for your infants, toddlers, teens, young adults, and grown-ups living on their own with children! Our need for God's wise plan in raising our children never stops, no matter their age. We need Him to guide us in raising our children. And as they grow, we need more and more wisdom to help guide them.

The good news? You and your children share in God's wise plan. Hallelujah!

Journal

Think of a time when you felt God's great wisdom.

Remember:

"We share in God's wise plan."

Day 12

Yet hope returns when I remember this one thing: The Lord's unfailing love and mercy still continue, fresh as the morning, as sure as the sunrise. The Lord is all I have, and so in Him I put my hope. (Lamentations 3:21–24 Good News Translation)

Kids tucked in bed. So tired. BUT, laundry to finish, bills to pay, backpacks to check, J.J. needs a class snack tomorrow, and…

"Mommy, I'm scared."

I snuggle in the rocking chair with J.J. on my lap. The storm rages outside, but in our corner of the world, love reigns. Everything that was so overwhelming minutes ago suddenly doesn't seem so important. Tomorrow is time enough.

His love is new every morning. Thank you, Jesus.

Journal

One thing I need to remember...

Remember:

"The Lord is all I have, and so in Him I put my hope."

Day 13

Leave all your worries with Him, because He cares for you. (I Peter 5:7, Good News Translation)

I love the visual this scripture brings to my mind—"LEAVE ALL your worries." I see myself walking up to Jesus, dropping my troubles, and then walking away lighter and happier. Seems so easy, doesn't it?

The more we practice, the easier it gets. So let's practice. Leave your cares at the feet of Jesus. Don't look back, AND don't grab them back. Just leave them. And then thank Him as you walk away.

Journal

Put your worries in the can, and leave them there!

Remember:

"Leave your worries."

Day 14

Freedom is what we have—Christ has set us free! Stand, then, as free people, and do not allow yourselves to become slaves again. (Galatians 5:1, Good News Translation)

It is difficult to admit we are slaves to something. We need to examine our lives. To what innocent and seemingly harmless things are we slaves? Are we enslaved by others' opinions of our parenting, of how our kids act, of how successful we are, of how athletic we are, of _____ (you fill in the blank)?

We all want people to see us and our children through our eyes, but we can't be enslaved to others' opinions. Only God's opinion should matter to us. Our goal is to be enslaved to His thoughts about our lives and our family.

Take a breath; you are a good MOM. Be free to believe it!

Journal

Make two lists, first list your areas of freedom; second, list areas in which you need God's help.

Remember:

"Freedom is what we (you) have."

Day 15

So now there is no condemnation for those who belong to Christ Jesus. (Romans 8:1, New Living Translation)

I was thinking of all the things in the world that could cause a mom to feel condemnation. The behavior of her children, whether they are toddlers, teens, or adults? What about being a working mom? The shame from finding it impossible to get everything finished? I could go on and on, but I don't want to concentrate on condemnation.

Do you belong to JESUS? If so, there is no condemnation. Love your kids, big or little. Leave the dishes in the sink and the laundry unfolded. And love your Lord by loving your family!

Journal

Make a list of things that would cause you to feel condemned. Take a marker and write "JESUS" over all of them!

Remember:

"There is no condemnation for those who belong to Jesus."

Day 16

Not that I speak from [any personal] need, for I have learned to be content [and self-sufficient through Christ, satisfied to the point where I am not disturbed or uneasy], regardless of my circumstances. (Philippians 4:11, Amplified Bible)

These words in the Amplified Bible stood out to me—"I am not disturbed or uneasy." As Moms, there are so many circumstances that pull at us. Toddlers, school-age children, teens, young adults, and adult children all needing or asking for our attention and time.

Stop! Crawl up onto Jesus' lap. No matter what is going on around us, it doesn't matter. Because of Jesus, we have what we need in ALL circumstances.

Journal

List the "God-circumstances" in your daily life.

Remember:

"I have learned to be content, regardless of my circumstances."

Day 17

I'll be with you as you do this day after day, after day, right up to the end of the age. (Matthew 28:20, The Message)

I love this translation—"day after day, after day." Not that all moms have things they do day after day, after day, but the first moms who popped into my head are the moms of toddlers and preschoolers. They spend their time training their children, day after day after day, without seeing immediate results.

But this verse says to me, "If your heart is for Me, I am with you day after day after day." Wiping noses, picking up toys, changing diapers, or answering 20,000 questions—HE IS WITH YOU.

Journal

As you go about the many, many tasks of being a mom today, tell HIM what it means to you to have HIM with you.

Remember:

"I'll be with you day after day, after day."

Day 18

> The law says we are under a curse for not always obeying it. But Christ took away that curse. He changed places with us and put Himself under that curse. Because of what Jesus Christ did, the blessing God promised to Abraham was given to ALL people. Christ died so that by believing in Him we could have the Spirit that God promised. (Galatians 3:13-14, Easy-to-Read Version)

Two things hit me when I read this verse. First, as Moms, no matter what age our children are, we always think we could have/should have done things differently/better. God says that is not so.

And second, God loves me so much that He would trade places for me and give up His only Son. What Mom doesn't want to take on the trials and burdens of their child, no matter what age?

GOOD NEWS! God has already taken care of us moms AND our kids. Thank you, Jesus!

Journal

List His blessings in your life.

Remember:

"He took away the curse. He changed places with us."

Day 19

Don't be obsessed with getting more material things. Be relaxed with what you have. Since God assured us, "I'll never let you down, never walk off and leave you," we can boldly quote: God is there, ready to help; I'm fearless no matter what. (Hebrews 13:5-6, The Message)

"Never walk off and leave you" and "I'm fearless"–those could be definitions of a MOM. We are fearless when defending our children, whether it is a two-year-old in the midst of a tantrum, a teen with a need for guidance, or an adult child who needs your help. But know that you must pray and let God lead them.

Now, who loves us when we throw a tantrum, have an attitude, or think we know what to do without asking for help? Hmmmm, I see myself in all those situations. OUCH!

But His love for me never wavers. He will never let me down. He is fearless. I'm thankful!

Journal

List the times you have seen, in spite of your attitude, God's faithfulness in your life.

Remember:

"I'll...never leave you...I'm FEARLESS."

Day 20

For God is not a God of disorder but of peace-as in all the congregations of the Lord's people. (I Corinthians 14:33 New International Version)

I like order and peace in life and in our home. It is comforting to me to hear God say He likes it too. We have the power to bring peace to our toddlers, teens, and adult children. A simple hug, message in a lunch bag, text, phone call, or smile tells them, "All is well; be at peace." You are a peacemaker in your home. Let peace begin with you.

Journal

Listen to the song "Let There Be Peace on Earth."
What is He saying to you?

Remember:

"God is a God of peace."

Day 21

I've said these things to you so that you will have peace in Me. In the world you have distress. But be encouraged! I have conquered the world. (John 16:33, Common English Bible)

Every translation of this verse spoke to me. Here are some of the words God highlighted to me from other translations–*encouraged, brave, peace, take heart, courageous, undaunted, joyful, victorious, and cheerful.* As we end this twenty-one day journey, He wants to say to you, "You are brave, you are victorious, you are cheerful, you are courageous, you are joyful." Being a MOM is the single, most important, life-changing job you could ever have. And HE is right beside you, overcoming the world...FOR YOU.

Thank you for walking this twenty-one day *MOM CAN* journey with me. What I thought would be an easy devotional to write turned out to be the hardest. I pray these are His words for every MOM.

Journal

What has God shown you that you CAN do?

Remember:

"He has overcome the world."

MOM "CANS"

Day 1
Light a CAN-dle.

Day 2
CAN-cel something that isn't important.

Day 3
Spend some time with a CAN-ine friend.

Day 4
Think of your life as a blank CAN-vas. What would you draw?

Day 5
Bake a cake using CAN-ola oil!

Day 6
Fill up a CAN-teen and go for a walk.

Day 7
Have you ever thought about being a CAN-didate for office?

Day 8
Pray for healing someone you know who has CAN-cer.

Day 9
Have a CAN-did conversation with a friend.

Day 10
Eat CAN-taloupe.

Day 11
Learn how to play CAN-asta.

Day 12
Take a CAN-oe trip.

Day 13

Walk along a CAN-al.

Day 14

Eat dinner by CAN-dlelight.

Day 15

Have a seat under a CAN-opy.

Day 16

Hike in a CAN-yon.

Day 17

Dance the CAN-CAN!

Day 18

Be a CAN-tor (sing).

Day 19

Go out and CAN-ter (trot).

Day 20

Go to a pet store and watch the CAN-aries.

Day 21

Eat your favorite CAN-dy.

We all take ourselves so seriously. Each day, remember you CAN laugh, you CAN take time for yourself, and you CAN do something you enjoy. You CAN be yourself—that's who God intended for you to be all along!

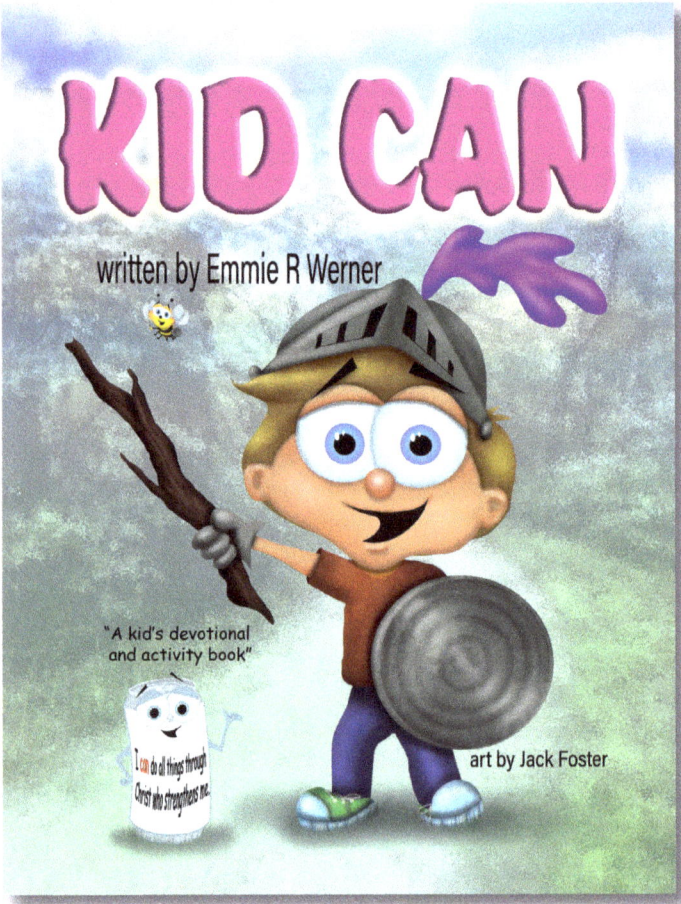

Kid Can

ISBN Paperback: 978-1-63765-046-2

Teen Can

ISBN Paperback: 978-1-63765-186-5

www.ingramcontent.com/pod-product-compliance
Lightning Source LLC
LaVergne TN
LVHW070012090426

835509LV00041B/3476